BEAR
BONES

ISBN 978-0-9838923-0-4

For you-know-who-you-are.

BEAR BONES

by Gary Bueno

www.garybueno.com

YAAAAAWWN

SCRATCH
SCRATCH
SCRATCH
SCRATCH

DO NOT
FEED
BEARS

CAUTION

www.ingramcontent.com/pod-product-compliance
Lightning Source LLC
Chambersburg PA
CBHW071420040426
42445CB00012BA/1232
9780983892304